CHRISTMAS
100 SEASONAL FAVORITES

P9-CRZ-570

HAL LEONARD PUBLISHING CORPORATION

Home Office:
960 East Mark Street
Winona MN 55987

National Sales Office:
8112 West Bluemound Road
Milwaukee WI 53213

A CAROLING WE GO

Words and Music by JOHNNY MARKS

Moderately bright

A car - ol - ing, a car - ol - ing, A Car - ol - ing We Go,
bring you sea - son's greet - ings and we wish the best to you,

Hearts filled with mu - sic and cheeks a - glow. From
And may our wish last the whole year through. Come

house to house we bring the mes - sage of the King a - gain,
join us if you will as we are sing - ing once a - gain,

ALL THROUGH THE NIGHT

Traditional

ALMOST DAY
(It's Almost Day)

Words and Music by HUDDIE LEDBETTER

Square Dance Tempo

Chick - ens a - crowin' for mid - night, It's Al - most Day;

Chick - ens a - crowin' for mid - night, It's Al - most Day.

Can - dy canes___ and sug - ar plums,___ On Christ - mas day;

ANGELS FROM THE REALMS OF GLORY

Words by JAMES MONTGOMERY
Music by HENRY SMART

ANGELS WE HAVE HEARD ON HIGH

French-English

Moderately

An - gels we have heard on high Sweet - ly sing - ing

o'er the plains, And the moun - tains in re - ply

Ech - o - ing their joy - ous strains. Glo -

AULD LANG SYNE

Moderately

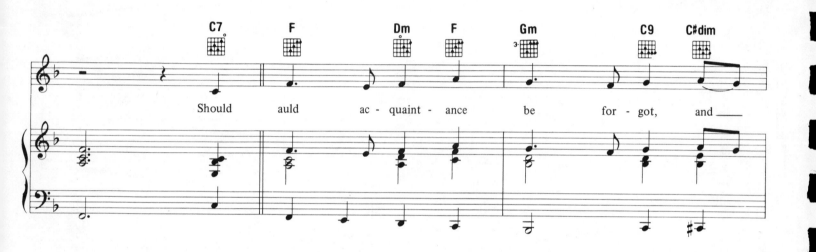

Should auld ac-quaint-ance be for-got, and ____

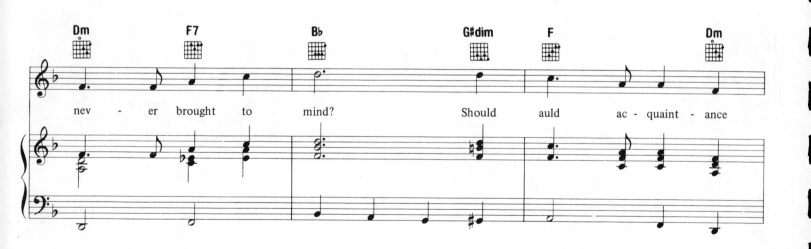

nev - er brought to mind? Should auld ac-quaint-ance

AWAY IN A MANGER

Words by MARTIN LUTHER
Music by CARL MUELLER

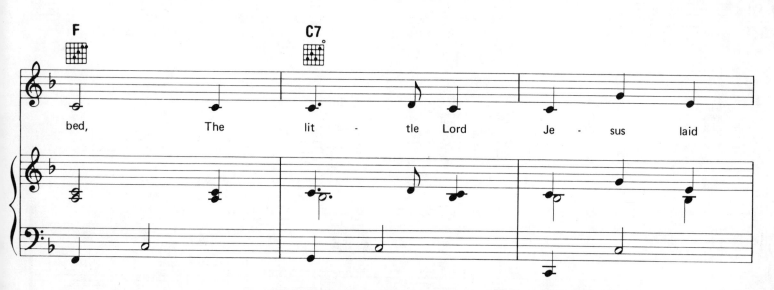

19

BURGUNDIAN CAROL

Words & Music by OSCAR BRAND

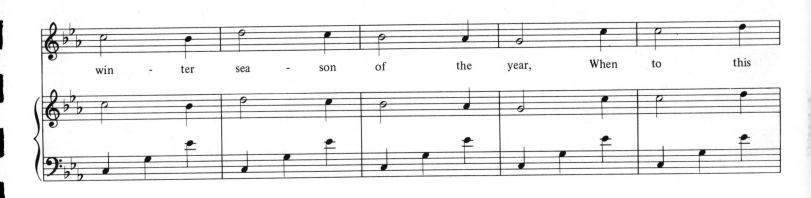

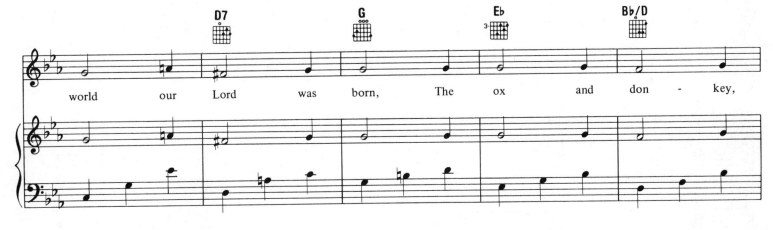

AWAY IN A MANGER

Words by MARTIN LUTHER
Music by JONATHAN E. SPILLMAN

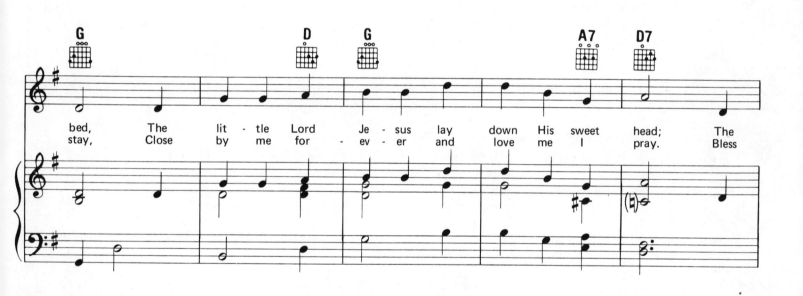

BLUE CHRISTMAS

Words by JAY W. JOHNSON
Music by BILLY HAYES

Slowly

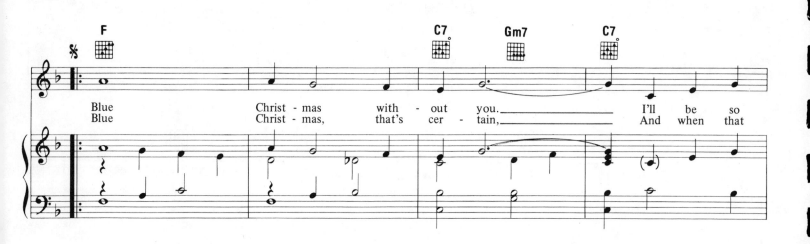

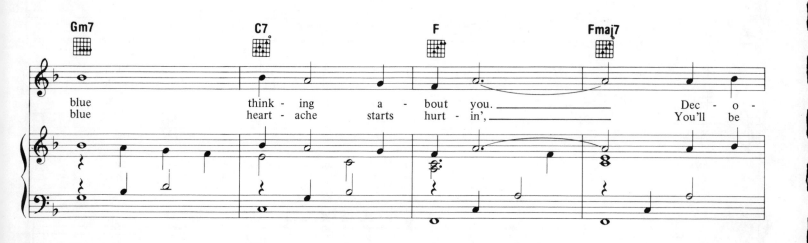

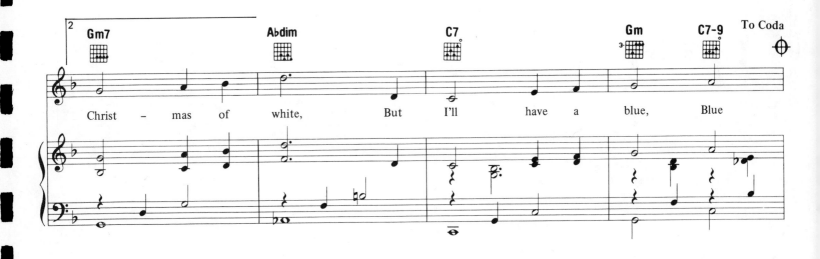

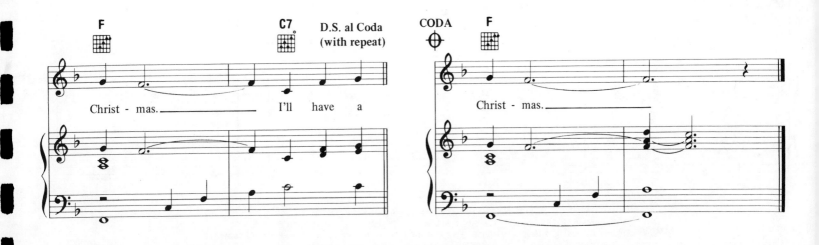

THE BOAR'S HEAD CAROL

English

With spirit

The boar's head in hand bear I, Be-decked with bays and rose-ma-ry. And I pray you, my mas-ters mer-ry be, Quot es-tes in con-vi-vi-o,

BRING A TORCH, JEANNETTE, ISABELLA

Provençal

Brightly

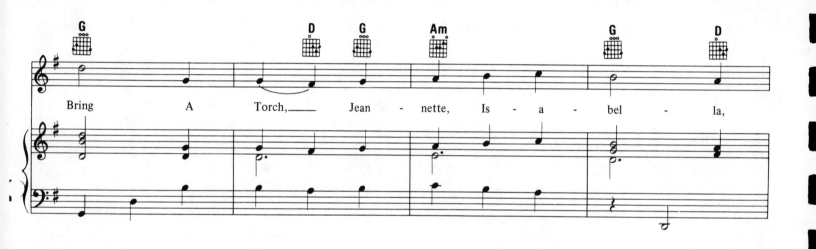

Bring A Torch,___ Jean - nette, Is - a - bel - la,

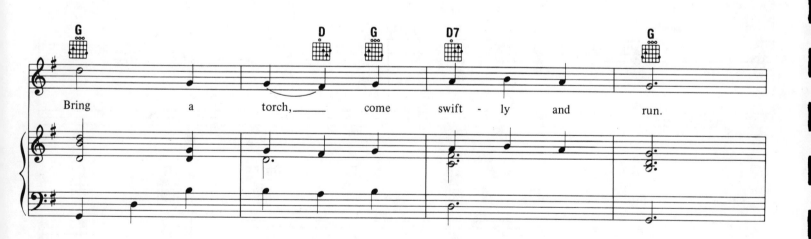

Bring a torch,___ come swift - ly and run.

Hasten now, good folk of the village,
Hasten now, the Christ Child to see.
You will find him asleep in a manger,
Quietly come and whisper softly,
Hush, hush, Peacefully now He slumbers,
Hush, hush, Peacefully now He sleeps.

C-H-R-I-S-T-M-A-S

Moderato (with expression)

Words by JENNY LOU CARSON
Music by EDDY ARNOLD

33

CAROL OF THE BELLS

Exuberantly

Ukranian

Hark to the bells, hark to the bells,

tell - ing us all Je - sus is King! Strong - ly they chime, sound with a rhyme,

CAROLING, CAROLING

Words by WIHLA HUTSON
Music by ALFRED BURT

THE CHIPMUNK SONG

Words and Music by
ROSS BAGDASARIAN

CHRIST WAS BORN ON CHRISTMAS DAY

German

41

THE CHRISTMAS WALTZ

Lyric by SAMMY CAHN
Music by JULE STYNE

THE COVENTRY CAROL

English, 16th Century

3. Herod the king,
   In his raging,
   Charged he hath this day.
   His men of might,
   In his own sight,
   All young children to slay.

4. That woe is me,
   Poor child for thee!
   And ever morn and day,
   For thy parting
   Neither say nor sing
   By by, lully lullay!

DANCE OF THE SUGAR PLUM FAIRY

By P.I. TCHAIKOVSKY

DECK THE HALL

Welsh

la la la la. Don we now our gay ap-par - el,
la la la la. Fol - low me in mer - ry mea - sure,
la la la la. Sing we joy - ous, all to-geth - er

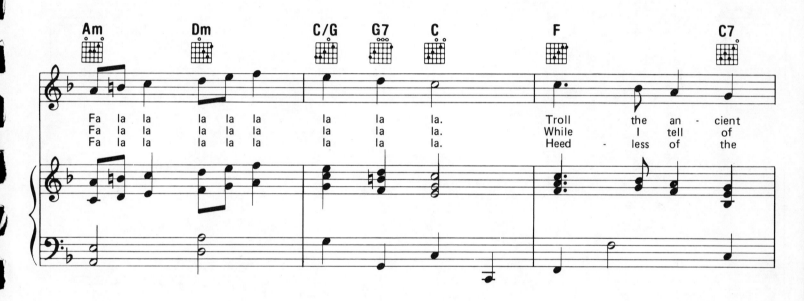

Fa la la la la la la la la la. Troll the an - cient
Fa la la la la la la la la la. While I tell of
Fa la la la la la la la la la. Heed - less of the

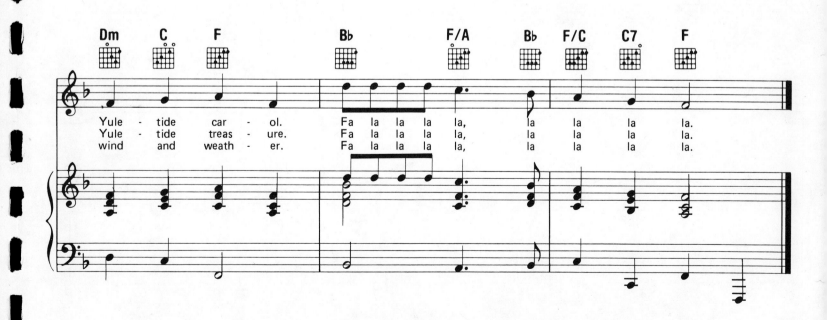

Yule - tide car - ol. Fa la la la la, la la la la.
Yule - tide treas - ure. Fa la la la la, la la la la.
wind and weath - er. Fa la la la la, la la la la.

DO THEY KNOW IT'S CHRISTMAS?

Medium Rock

Words and Music by
M. URE and B. GELDOF

49

THE FRIENDLY BEASTS

Moderately

English

2. "I," said the donkey, shaggy and brown,
"I carried His mother up hill and down;
I carried her safely to Bethlehem town."
"I," said the donkey, shaggy and brown.

3. "I," said the cow all white and red,
"I gave Him my manger for His bed;
I gave Him my hay to pillow His head."
"I," said the cow all white and red.

4. "I," said the sheep with curly horn,
"I gave Him my wool for His blanket warm;
He wore my coat on Christmas morn."
"I," said the sheep with curly horn.

5. "I," said the dove from the rafters high,
"I cooed Him to sleep so He would not cry,
We cooed Him to sleep, my mate and I."
"I," said the dove from the rafter high.

6. Thus every beast by some good spell,
In the stable dark was glad to tell
Of the gift he gave Emanuel,
The gift he gave Emanuel.

THE FIRST NOEL

French-English

2. They looked up and saw a star
Shining in the East, beyond them far;
And to the earth it gave great light,
And so it continued both day and night.

Refrain

3. And by the light of that same star,
Three wise men came from country far;
To seek for a King was their intent,
And to follow the star wherever it went.

Refrain

4. This star drew night to the northwest,
O'er Bethlehem it took its rest;
And there it did both stop and stay,
Right over the place where Jesus lay.

Refrain

5. Then entered in those wise men three,
Full reverently upon their knee;
And offered there in His presence,
Their gold, and myrrh, and frankincense.

Refrain

FROSTY THE SNOW MAN

Words and Music by
STEVE NELSON
and JACK ROLLINS

Moderato

1. FROS - TY, THE SNOW MAN was a jol - ly hap - py soul,___ With a
2. FROS - TY, THE SNOW MAN knew the sun was hot that day,___ So he

corn cob pipe and a but - ton nose___ and two eyes made out of coal.
said "Let's run and we'll have some fun___ now be - fore I melt a - way."

GESU BAMBINO
(The Infant Jesus)

By PIETRO A. YON

Slowly

When
Nel

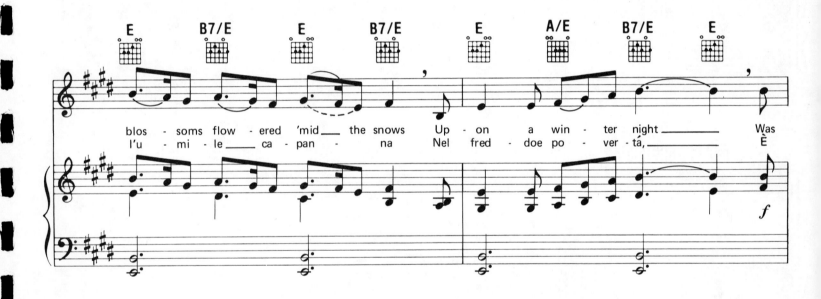

blos - soms flow - ered 'mid___ the snows   Up - on   a   win - ter night_____   Was
l'u - mi - le___ ca - pan - na   Nel fred - doe po - ver - tà,_____   È

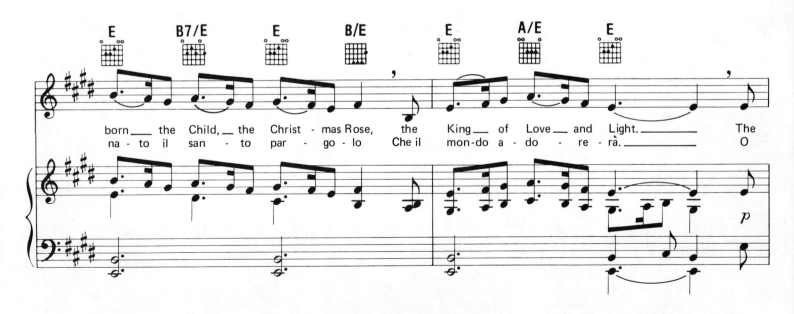

born___ the Child,___ the Christ - mas Rose,   the   King___ of Love___ and   Light.   The
na - to il san - to par - go - lo   Che il   mon - do a - do - re - rà.___   O

61

GO, TELL IT ON THE MOUNTAIN

Negro Spiritual

GOD REST YE MERRY, GENTLEMEN

Moderately

English

God Rest Ye Mer - ry Gen - tle - men, Let
In Beth - le - hem, in Jew - ry This

noth - ing you dis - may, For Je - sus Christ our
bless - ed babe was born, And laid with - in a

Sav - ior was born up - on this day, To
man - ger, Up - on this bless - ed morn; To

GOIN' ON A SLEIGHRIDE

Words and Music by
RALPH BLANE

69

GOOD CHRISTIAN MEN, REJOICE

German, 14th Century
Words translated by JOHN M. NEALE

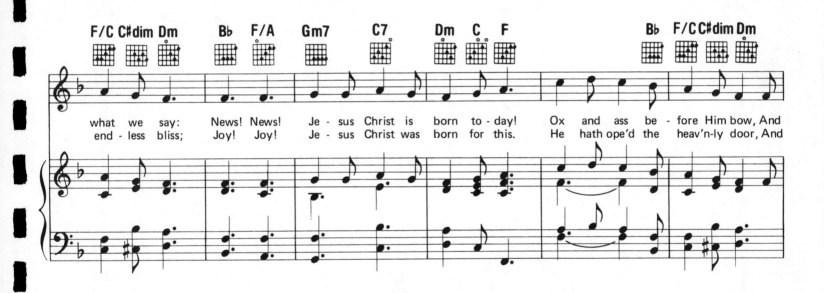

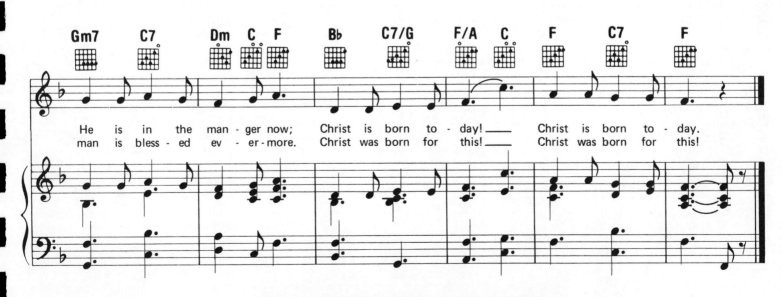

GOOD KING WENCESLAS

Words by JOHN M. NEALE
Traditional Melody

2.
"Hither page, and stand by me,
  If thou know'st it, telling,
Yonder peasant, who is he?
  Where and what his dwelling?"
"Sire, he lives a good league hence,
  Underneath the mountain;
Right against the forest fence,
  By Saint Agnes' fountain."

3.
"Bring me flesh, and bring me wine,
  Bring me pine-logs hither;
Thou and I will see him dine,
  When we bear them thither."
Page and monarch forth they went,
  Forth they went together;
Through the rude winds wild lament:
  And the bitter weather.

4.
"Sire, the night is darker now,
  And the wind blows stronger;
Fails my heart, I know not how,
  I can go not longer."
"Mark my footsteps, my good page,
  Tread thou in them boldly:
Thou shalt find the winter's rage
  Freeze thy blood less coldly."

5.
In his master's steps he trod,
  Where the snow lay dinted;
Heat was in the very sod
  Which the saint had printed.
Therefore, Christain men, be sure,
  Wealth or rank possessing,
Ye who now will bless the poor,
  Shall yourselves find blessing.

THE GREATEST GIFT OF ALL

Words and Music by JOHN JARVIS

78

A HOLLY JOLLY CHRISTMAS

Moderately bright with a happy feeling

Words and Music by JOHNNY MARKS

HARD CANDY CHRISTMAS

Words and Music by
CAROL HALL

HARK! THE HERALD ANGELS SING

Words by CHARLES WESLEY
Music by FELIX MENDELSSOHN-BARTHOLDY

HE

Words by Richard Mullen
Music by Jack Richards

HERE WE COME A-WASSAILING

English

Gaily

Here we come a-was-sail-ing A-mong the leaves so green;
We are not dai-ly beg-gars that beg from door to door,

Here we come a-wan-d'ring, So fair to be seen.
But we are neigh-bor chil-dren whom you have seen be-fore:

Love and joy come to you, And to you your was-sail

3. We have got a little purse
   Of stretching leather skin;
   We want a little money
   To line it well within:

4. God bless the master of this house,
   Likewise the mistress too;
   And all the little children
   That round the table go:

THE HOLLY AND THE IVY

French

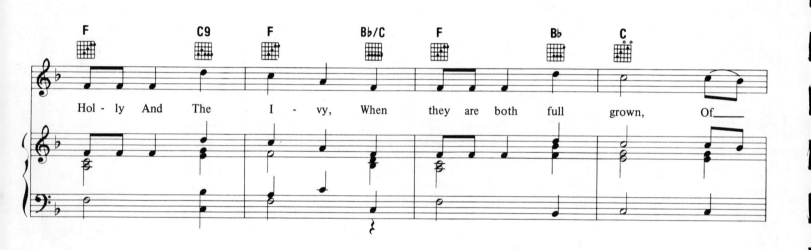

95

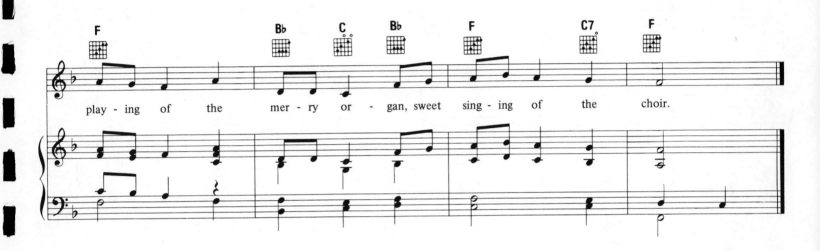

2. The holly bears a blossom,
As white as lily flow'r,
And Mary bore sweet Jesus Christ,
To be our sweet Saviour.

Refrain

3. The holly bears a berry,
As red as any blood,
And Mary bore sweet Jesus Christ,
To do poor sinners good.

Refrain

(There's No Place Like)
HOME FOR THE HOLIDAYS

Words by AL STILLMAN
Music by ROBERT ALLEN

Moderato, With Feeling

I HEARD THE BELLS ON CHRISTMAS DAY

Words by HENRY WADSWORTH LONGFELLOW
Music by JOHN BAPTISTE CALKIN

3. And in despair I bow'd my head:
   "There is no peace on earth," I said,
   "For hate is strong, and mocks the song
   Of peace on earth, good will to men."

4. Then pealed the bells more loud and deep:
   "God is not dead, nor doth He sleep;
   The wrong shall fail, the right prevail,
   With peace on earth, good will to men."

5. Till, ringing, singing on its way,
   The world revolved from night to day,
   A voice, a chime, a chant sublime,
   Of peace on earth, good will to men!

I HEARD THE BELLS ON CHRISTMAS DAY

Words by HENRY LONGFELLOW
Adapted by JOHNNY MARKS
Music by JOHNNY MARKS

Moderately slow

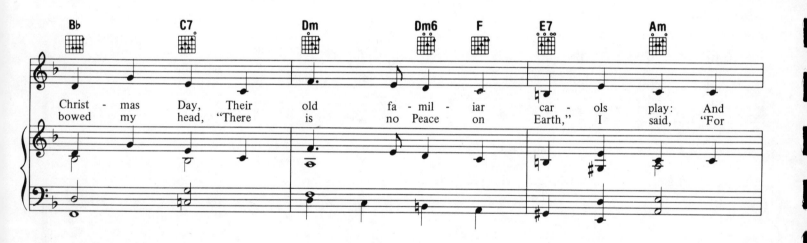

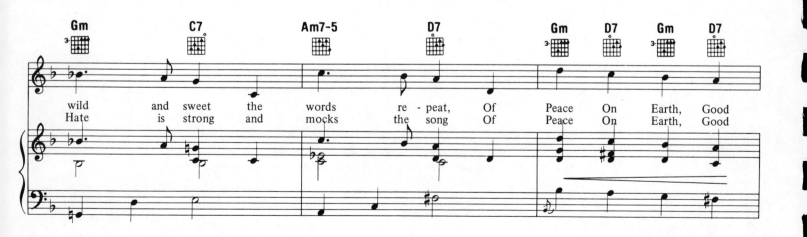

I SAW MOMMY KISSING SANTA CLAUS

Words and Music by
TOMMIE CONNOR

Moderately slow

I saw Mom-my kiss-ing San - ta Claus, un-der-neath the mis-tle-toe last night._____ She did-n't see me creep down the stairs to have a peep, she thought that I was tucked up in my bed-room fast a-

I SAW THREE SHIPS

English

I'LL BE HOME FOR CHRISTMAS

Words and Music by
KIM GANNON, WALTER KENT
and BUCK RAM

Moderately slow

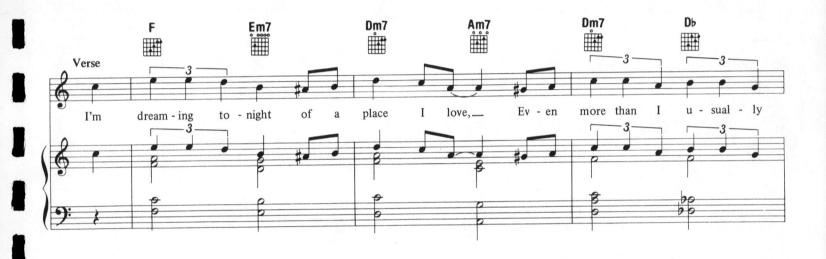

Verse

I'm dream-ing to-night of a place I love,___ Ev-en more than I u-sual-ly

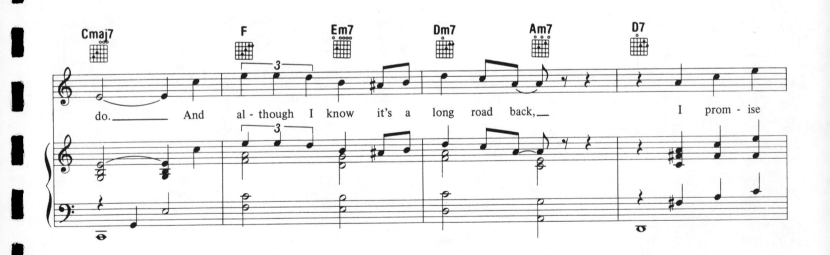

do._____ And al-though I know it's a long road back,___ I prom-ise

106

IT CAME UPON THE MIDNIGHT CLEAR

Words by EDMUND H. SEARS
Music by RICHARD S. WILLIS

109

110

JESU, JOY OF MAN'S DESIRING

By J.S. BACH

113

Thee, our souls as - pir - ing,
flock in Thee con - fid - ing,

Soar to un - cre -
Drink of joy from

at - ed light.
death - less springs.

114

JINGLE-BELL ROCK

Words and Music by
JOE BEAL
and JIM BOOTHE

Moderately (with a rock beat)

Chorus

Jin-gle-bell, Jin-gle-bell, JIN-GLE-BELL ROCK__ Jin-gle-bell swing and

Jin-gle-bells ring Snow-in' and blow-in' up bush-els of fun

117

JOLLY OLD ST. NICHOLAS

Traditional

JINGLE BELLS

Bright 2

Words and Music by
J. PIERPONT

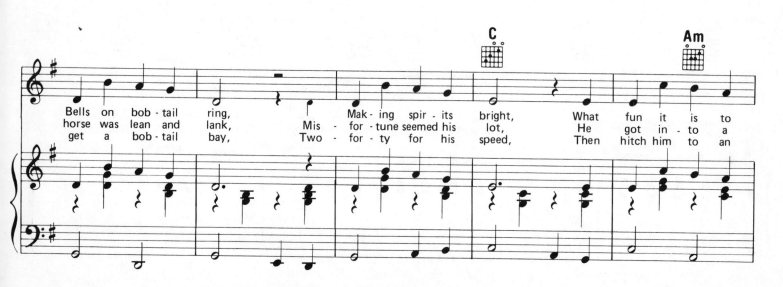

JINGLE JINGLE JINGLE

Words and Music by JOHNNY MARKS

Moderately, Gaily

Jin - gle, Jin - gle, Jin - gle, you will hear {my/his} sleigh bells ring,

{I am/Jol - ly} old Kris Krin - gle, {I'm/is} the King of jin - gl - ing

Jin - gle, jin - gle rein - deer, through the frost - y air they'll go, They are not just

JOY TO THE WORLD

Words by ISAAC WATTS
Music by GEORGE F. HANDEL

With spirit

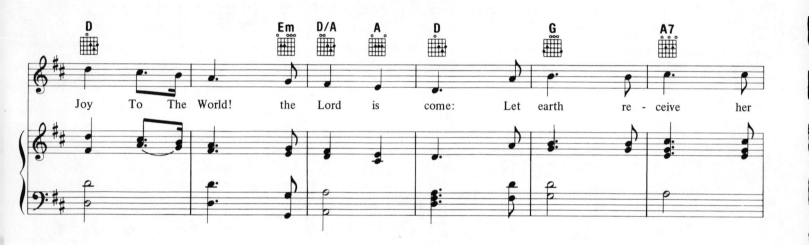

Joy To The World! the Lord is come: Let earth re-ceive her

King; Let ev-ery___ heart___ pre-pare Him___ room,___ And heaven and na-ture___

THE LAST MONTH OF THE YEAR
(What Month Was Jesus Born In?)

Words and Music by VERA HALL
Adapted and Arranged by
RUDY PICKENS TARTT and ALAN LOMAX

What month___ was my Je - sus born___ in?
Well, they laid___ Him in a man - ger, } Last month___ of the year!

What month___ was my Je - sus born___ in?
Well, they laid___ Him in the man - ger, } Last month___ of the year!___ Oh,

Jan - u - ar - y, Feb - ru - ar - y, March, _____

(Jan - u - ar - y) (Feb - ru - ar - y)

LITTLE TOWN

Words and Music by
CHRIS EATON

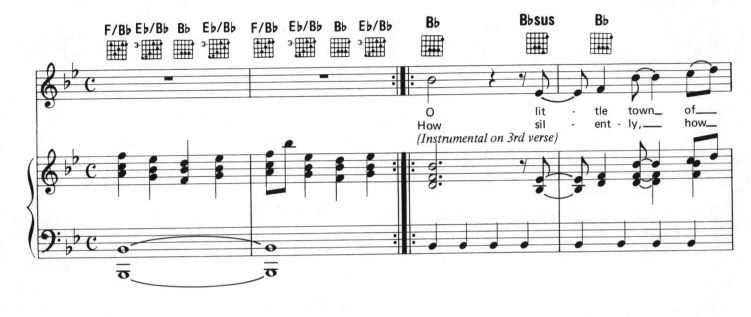

O lit - tle town_ of_
How sil - ent - ly,_ how
(Instrumental on 3rd verse)

Beth - le - hem_ how_ still we see
sil - ent - ly_ the_ wond - 'rous gift

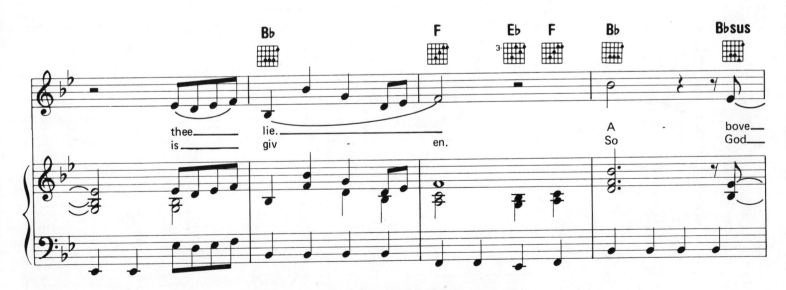

thee_ lie._ A - bove_
is_ giv - en. So_ God_

LET IT SNOW! LET IT SNOW! LET IT SNOW!

Words by SAMMY CAHN
Music by JULE STYNE

THE LITTLE DRUMMER BOY

Words and Music by KATHERINE DAVIS,
HENRY ONORATI and HARRY SIMEONE

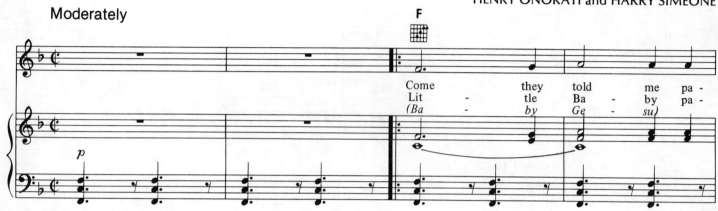

137

MARCH OF THE TOYS

With Spirit

By VICTOR HERBERT

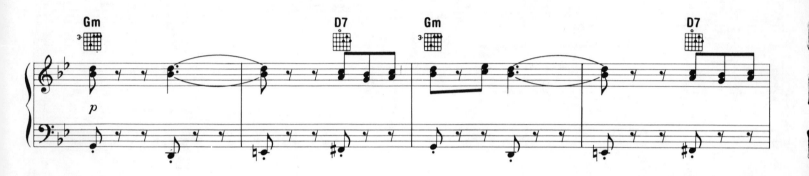

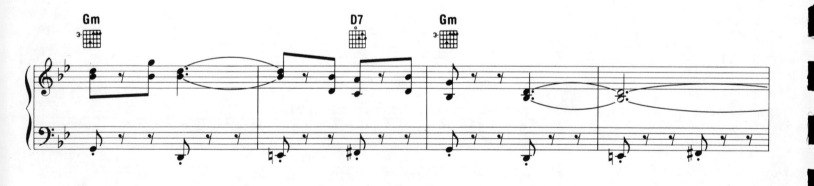

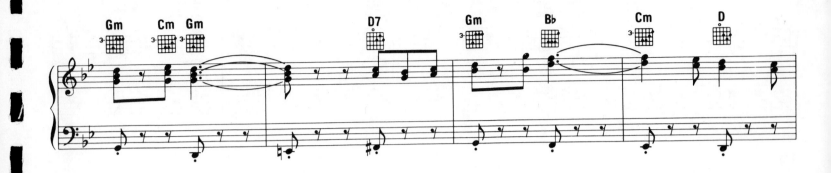

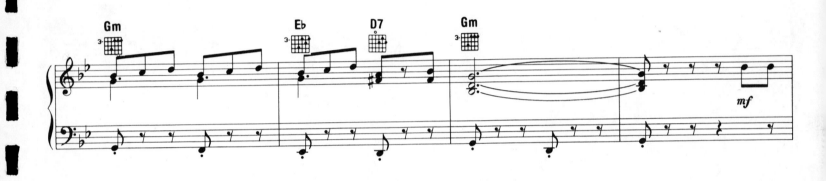

A MARSHMALLOW WORLD

Words by CARL SIGMAN
Music by PETER DE ROSE

MARY'S LITTLE BOY CHILD

By JESTER HAIRSTON

Slowly

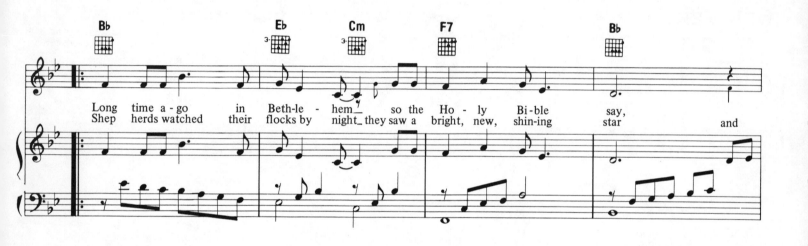

Long time a - go in Beth-le - hem so the Ho - ly Bi - ble say,
Shep herds watched in their flocks by night they saw a bright, new, shin-ing star and

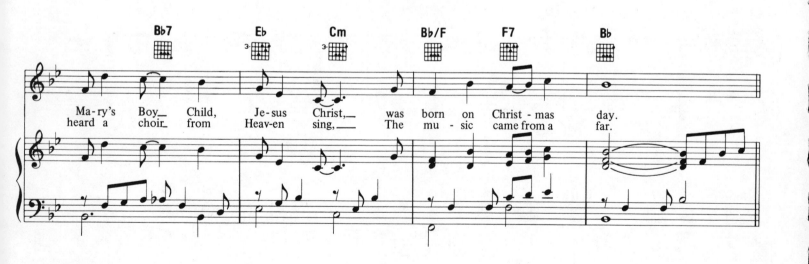

Ma-ry's Boy Child, Je - sus Christ, was born on Christ - mas day.
heard a choir from Heav-en sing, The mu - sic came from a far.

A MERRY, MERRY CHRISTMAS TO YOU

Words and Music by JOHNNY MARKS

*Use any language desired.

(*) Can repeat full chorus then 4 bar vamp shouting languages, then Coda.

THE MERRY CHRISTMAS POLKA

Words by PAUL FRANCIS WEBSTER
Music by SONNY BURKE

Moderately (Tempo di Polka)

They're tun - ing up the fid - dles now, the fid - dles now, the

fid - dles now, There's wine to warm the mid - dles now and set your head a -

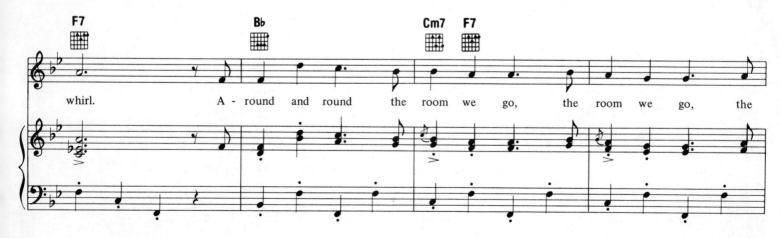

whirl. A - round and round the room we go, the room we go, the

153

THE MOST WONDERFUL DAY OF THE YEAR

Words and Music by JOHNNY MARKS

We're on the is - land of Mis - fit Toys,
Up at the North Pole they have fit their laws,

Here we
Elves must

don't want to stay.
work ev - 'ry day.

We want to trav - el with
Mak - ing the toys that old

San - ta Claus, in his mag - ic sleigh.
San - ta Claus loads up - on his sleigh.

MY FAVORITE THINGS
(From "THE SOUND OF MUSIC")

Words by OSCAR HAMMERSTEIN II
Music by RICHARD RODGERS

When the dog bites, When the bee stings,

When I'm feel- ing sad, _____ I sim- ply re-

-mem- ber my fa- vor- ite things and then I don't feel

so bad. _____

THE NIGHT BEFORE CHRISTMAS SONG

Words adapted by JOHNNY MARKS from CLEMENT MOORE'S Poem
Music by JOHNNY MARKS

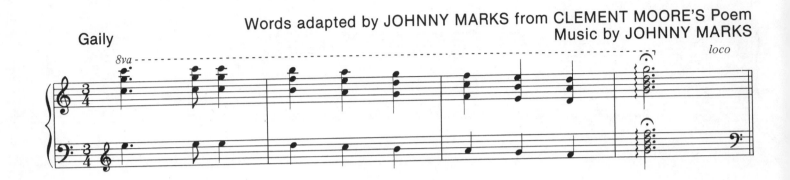

'Twas The Night Be-fore Christ-mas and all thru the house, not a crea-ture was
up to the house-top and the rein-deer soon flew, with the sleigh full of

stir - ring not e - ven a mouse. All the stock - ings were hung by the
toys and St. Nich - o - las too. Down the chim - ney he came with a

NOEL! NOEL!

French-English

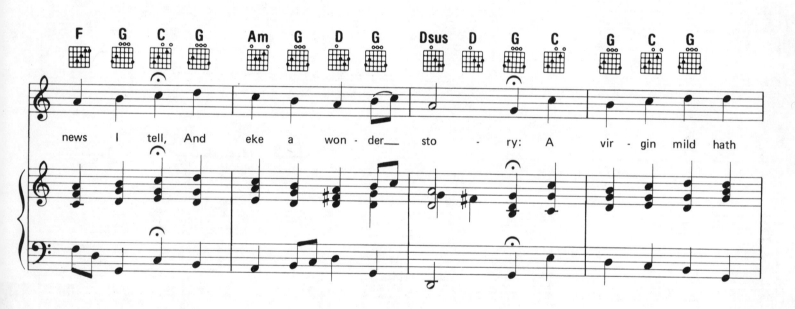

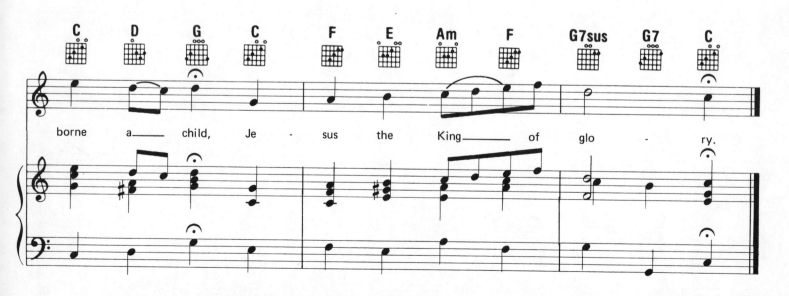

NUTTIN' FOR CHRISTMAS

Words and Music by
ROY BENNETT and SID TEPPER

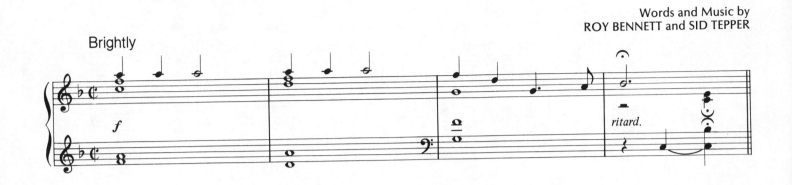

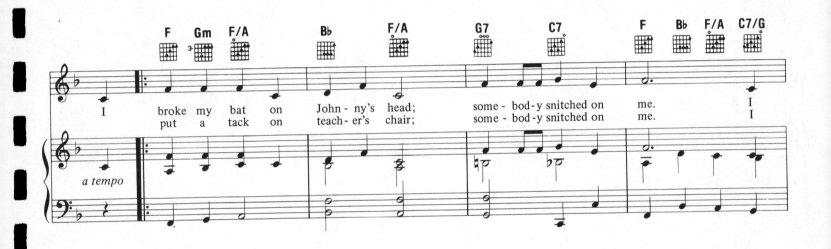

I
broke my bat on John - ny's head;
put a tack on teach - er's chair;
some - bod - y snitched on me.
some - bod - y snitched on me.
I

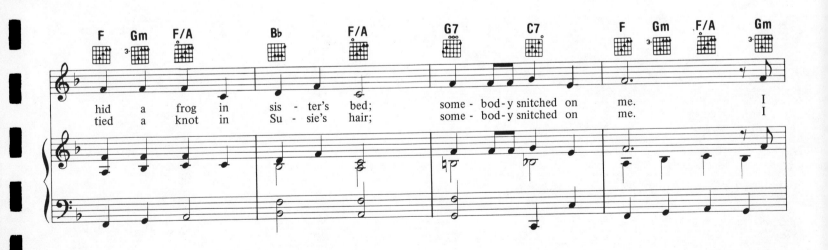

hid a frog in sis - ter's bed;
tied a knot in Su - sie's hair;
some - bod - y snitched on me.
some - bod - y snitched on me.
I

3. I won't be seeing Santa Claus; somebody snitched on me.
He won't come visit me because somebody snitched on me.
Next year I'll be going straight, next year I'll be good, just wait,
I'd start now but it's too late; somebody snitched on me. Oh,

O COME ALL YE FAITHFUL

Latin Words translated by
FREDERICK OAKELEY
Music by JOHN READING

O CHRISTMAS TREE

German

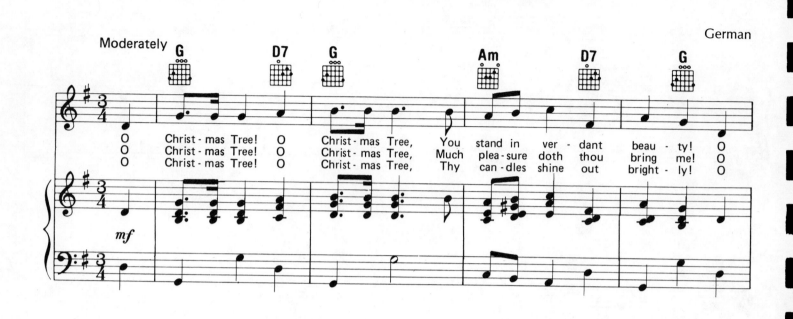

O COME, O COME, IMMANUEL

Plainsong, 13th Century
Words translated by JOHN M. NEALE and HENRY S. COFFIN

Like an old plainsong

O

Guitar tacet

Come, O Come Im - man - u - el, And

ran - som cap - tive Is - ra - el, That mourns in lone - ly

O HOLY NIGHT

English Words by J.S. DWIGHT
Music by ADOLPHE ADAM

O LITTLE TOWN OF BETHLEHEM

Words by PHILLIPS BROOKS
Music by LEWIS H. REDNER

OLD TOY TRAINS

Words and Music by
ROGER MILLER

Lit - tle toy___ trains,___ lit - tle toy___ tracks,___ lit - tle toy___ drums___ com - in' from a sack, car - ried by a man dressed in white and red. Lit - tle boy___ don't___ you think it's time you were in bed? Close your

181

O SANCTISSIMA

Joyfully

Sicilian

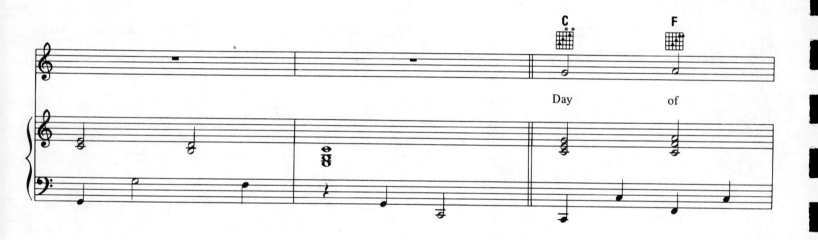

Day of

ho - li - ness,_____ peace and hap - pi - ness,_____

ONCE IN ROYAL DAVID'S CITY

Words by C.F. ALEXANDER
Music by H.J. GAUNTLETT

Quietly

Once In Roy - al

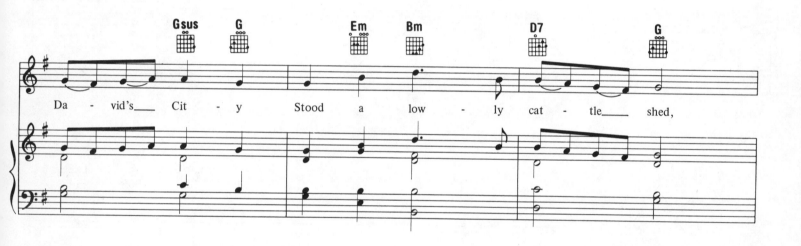

Da - vid's___ Cit - y Stood a low - ly cat - tle___ shed,

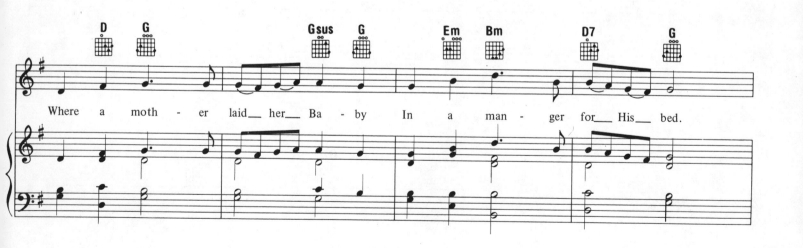

Where a moth - er laid___ her___ Ba - by In a man - ger for___ His___ bed.

PARADE OF THE WOODEN SOLDIERS

Words and Music by BALLARD MACDONALD
and LEON JESSEL

PRETTY PAPER

Words and Music by
WILLIE NELSON

190

R2D2, WE WISH YOU A MERRY CHRISTMAS

Words and Music by
MECO MONARDO and DON ORIOLO

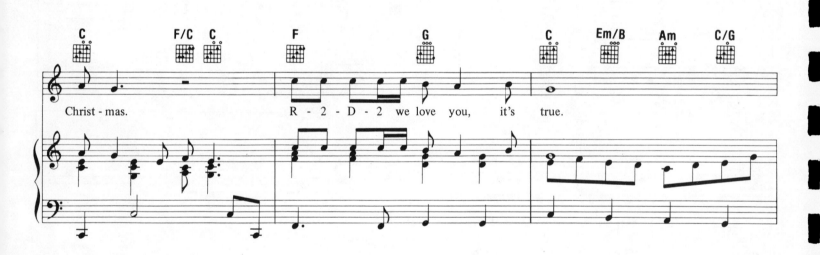

ROCKIN' AROUND THE CHRISTMAS TREE

Moderately with a Rock

Words and Music by JOHNNY MARKS

Rock-in' A-round The Christ-mas Tree___ at the Christ-mas par-ty hop.___

Mis-tle-toe hung where you can see___ ev-'ry

cou-ple tries to stop.

Rock-in' A-round The

boughs of hol - ly". Rock - in' A - round The Christ - mas Tree.__ Have a

hap - py hol - i - day.__ Ev - 'ry - one danc - ing mer - ri - ly__ in the

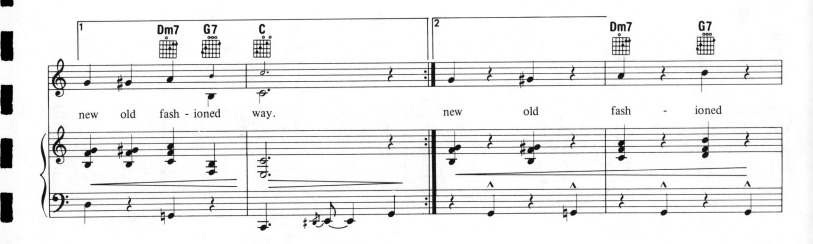

new old fash - ioned way. new old fash - ioned

way._____

RUDOLPH THE RED-NOSED REINDEER

Words and Music by JOHNNY MARKS

199

SANTA, BRING MY BABY BACK
(To Me)

Words and Music by
CLAUDE DeMETRIUS and AARON SCHROEDER

Bright rock

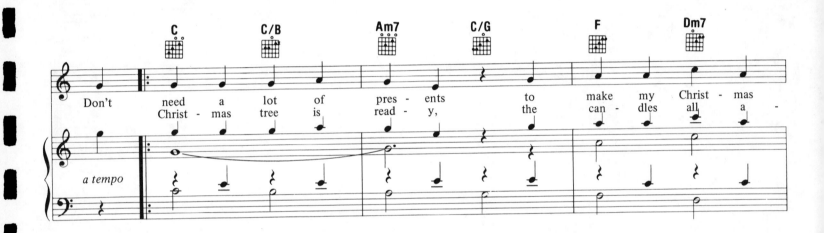

Don't need a lot of pres- ents, to make my Christ- mas
Christ- mas tree is read- y, the can- dles all a-

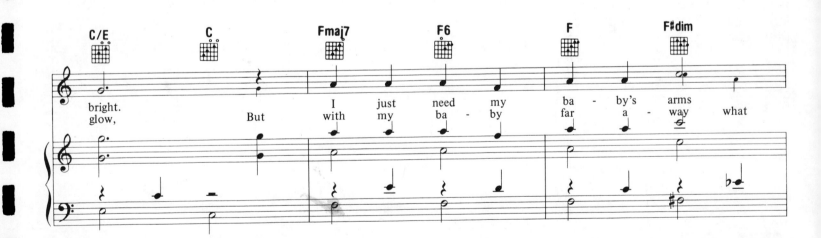

bright. But I just need my ba- by's arms
glow, with my ba- by far a- way what

202

SILENT NIGHT

Words by JOSEPH MOHR
Music by FRANZ GRÜBER

SILVER AND GOLD

Slowly and expressively

Words and Music by JOHNNY MARKS

Sil - ver And Gold, Sil - ver And Gold, Ev - 'ry-one wish - es for Sil - ver And Gold, How do you meas - ure its worth?_____ Just by the pleas - ure it gives here on

207

SLEEP, HOLY BABE

Words by EDWARD CASWELL
Music by J.B. DYKES

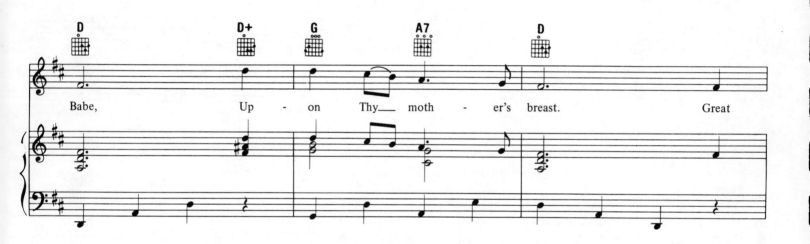

SLEIGH RIDE

Words by MITCHELL PARISH
Music by LEROY ANDERSON

212

SOME CHILDREN SEE HIM

Words by WIHLA HUTSON
Music by ALFRED BURT

SUZY SNOWFLAKE

Words and Music by
SID TEPPER and ROY BENNETT

THE STAR CAROL

Words by WIHLA HUTSON
Music by ALFRED BURT

TOYLAND

Words by GLEN MAC DONOUGH
Music by VICTOR HERBERT

Lilting Waltz

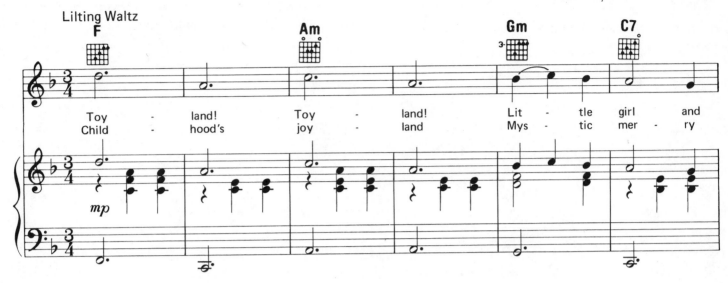

Toy - land! Toy - land! Lit - tle girl and
Child - hood's joy - land Mys - tic mer - ry

boy - land, While you dwell with - in it.____ You are ev - er hap - py
joy - land, Once you pass its

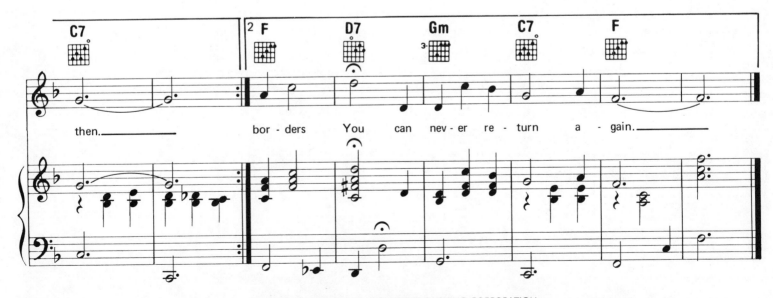

then._____ bor - ders You can nev - er re - turn a - gain._____

THAT CHRISTMAS FEELING

Words and Music by
BENNIE BENJAMIN and GEORGE WEISS

Moderately slow

THERE IS NO CHRISTMAS LIKE A HOME CHRISTMAS

Words by CARL SIGMAN
Music by MICKEY J. ADDY

THE TWELVE DAYS OF CHRISTMAS

UP ON THE HOUSE-TOP

Traditional

Brightly

Up on the house - top__ rein - deer pause,
First comes the stock - ing of lit - tle Nell;

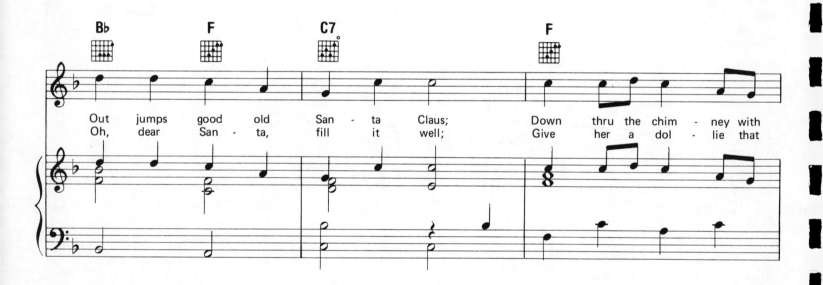

Out jumps good old San - ta Claus;
Oh, dear good San - ta, fill it well;

Down thru the chim - ney with
Give her a dol - lie that

lots of toys, All for the lit - tle ones, Christ - mas joys.}
laughs and cries, One that will o - pen and shut her eyes.}

Ho, ho, ho! Who would-n't go! Ho, ho, ho!

Who would-n't go!_____ Up on the house - top, click, click, click,

Down thru the chim - ney with good Saint Nick.

WE THREE KINGS OF ORIENT ARE

Words and Music by
JOHN H. HOPKINS

Moderately

We Three Kings of O - ri - ent are;

Bear - ing gifts we tra - verse a - far,

Field and foun - tain, moor and moun - tain,

WE WISH YOU A MERRY CHRISTMAS

Brightly

English

We wish you a Merry Christ-mas, We wish you a Mer-ry Christ-mas, We

wish you a Mer-ry Christ-mas, and a hap-py New Year. Good

WHEN SANTA CLAUS GETS YOUR LETTER

Words and Music by JOHNNY MARKS

WHAT CHILD IS THIS?

English

Slow and Serene

What Child is this,_____ who, laid to rest,_____ On
So bring Him in - cense, gold and myrrh,_____ Come

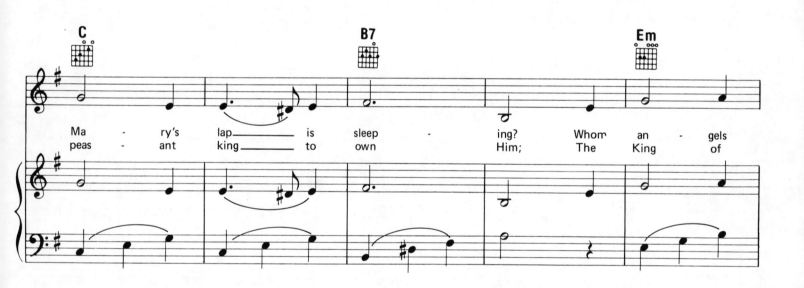

Ma - ry's lap_____ is sleep - ing? Whom an - gels
peas - ant king_____ to own Him; The King of

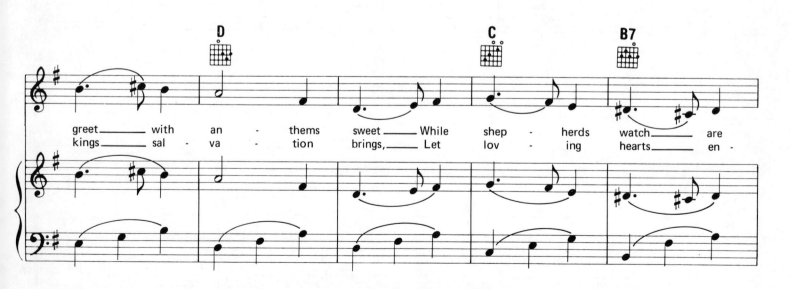

greet_____ with an - thems sweet_____ While shep - herds watch_____ are
kings_____ sal - va - tion brings,_____ Let lov - ing hearts_____ en -

WHILE SHEPHERDS WATCHED THEIR FLOCKS BY NIGHT

Words by NAHUM TATE
Music by GEORGE F. HANDEL

THE WHITE WORLD OF WINTER

Words by MITCHELL PARISH
Music by HOAGY CARMICHAEL

Moderately with a lift

In this won - der - ful White World Of Win - ter
(In this) won - der - ful White World Of Win - ter

Dar - ling, we'll have a won - der - ful time;
Dar - ling, we'll have a won - der - ful time;

First, we'll ride side by side thru the hin - ter
If we prayed it would snow all this win - ter

YOU MAKE IT FEEL LIKE CHRISTMAS

Words and Music by
NEIL DIAMOND

YOU'RE ALL I WANT FOR CHRISTMAS

Words and Music by
GLEN MOORE and SEGER ELLIS

THE WONDERFUL WORLD OF CHRISTMAS

Words by CHARLES TOBIAS
Music by AL FRISCH

Moderately slow

With feeling

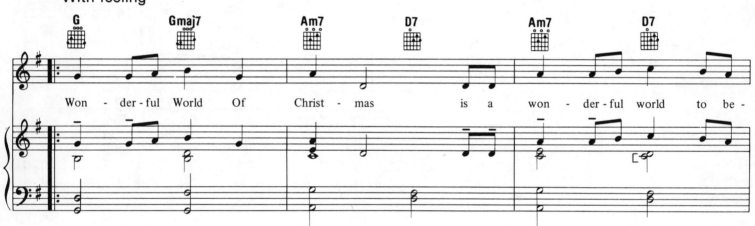

Won-der-ful World Of Christ-mas is a won-der-ful world to be-

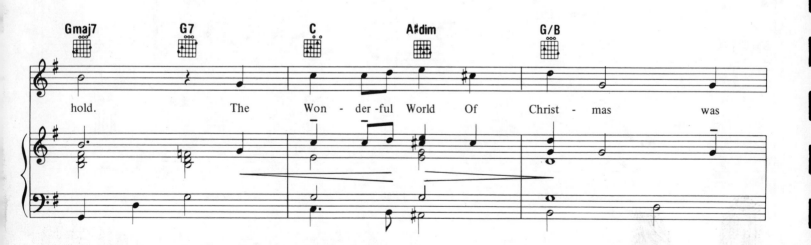

hold.   The Won-der-ful World Of Christ-mas was

248